LORO PARQUE

Nature's Paradise

Editor: Loro Parque S. A.

Design and Layout: Inge Feier and Ramón Jorge

Texts: Inge Feier

Copyright: Loro Parque S.A. 1998. The reproduction of this guidebook in any form, of the texts and photos contained herein is expressly prohibited without previous permission by the owners of the copyright.

Second Edition 2002

To request copies: Loro Parque S. A., 38400 Puerto de la Cruz (Tenerife), Canary Islands, Spain

Telephones: (34) 922 37 40 81 and (34) 922 37 38 41
Fax: (34) 922 37 50 21
E-mail: loroparque@loroparque.com
http: www:loroparque.com

Scanning: Fotomecánica Contacto, S.A.

Printed by: Litografía Romero, S.A.

Photos: Eumetsat, Tullio Gatti, Paul Salaman, Peter Oxford, Paul Reillo, Craig Symes

Illustrations: Tony Sánchez.

Depósito Legal: TF. 1.292-1998

ISBN: 84-930128-2-3

Bronze Cockatoos

The impressive bronze cockatoos at the entrance are the work of a renowned Thai artist. They are a symbol of the real treasure of LORO PARQUE: the Parrots.

Index

To all our friends,

I was 33 years old when I arrived in Puerto de la Cruz. That first impression of the mountains with their tall pine trees, the ever-present volcano and above all the friendliness of the people was all too much to resist. It was love at first sight.

On returning to Cologne, I spoke to my father about my plans for the future and he had the idea of creating a park for parrots in Tenerife. Loro Parque was born and on the 17th December 1972 we opened the gates of a park which then covered an area of 13.000 m² and which was to welcome more than 25 million visitors from that day to this. The park has never stopped growing, and today covers 10 times the original area. It houses within its walls the largest and most important parrot collection in the world with over 340 species and subspecies, which since 1994 has formed part of the LORO PARQUE FOUNDATION. One of the objects of the Foundation is to increase parrot populations with birds bred at the park and also to coordinate investigational studies in the countries of origin of these same birds which are often threatened with extinction.

All our efforts are centred on the upkeep of the parrot collection as we are very conscious of being the executors of an important heritage to mankind, especially in these times of deforestation, pollution and a decline in ethical and aesthetic standards. Our parrots are their own ambassadors for self-preservation, able to attract the attention and assistance they require from humans to achieve this.

When you are strolling through Loro Parque enjoying the fauna, remember that many of these species are threatened by extinction in their natural habitat. In the past century alone mankind has destroyed more than 60% of tropical forest.

For this reason there is a need for well-managed zoological installations which can help to save at least some part of the species which are endangered. It has already been possible to assure the survival of many such species by way of conservation projects. We rely on nature, but it also relies on us, and this should be the "reason to be" for Loro Parque and every other zoological park.

Loro Parque and Loro Parque Foundation are campaigners for the conservation of nature and we try to inform and educate the public in this respect. Our visitors therefore have the opportunity to become a true friend to nature and directly contribute to its protection.

The animals themselves are also helping their wild counterparts by fondly attracting the visitor's attention and interest. We try to bring you closer to nature and to our animals so that together we can preserve what God has created.

Welcome to LORO PARQUE; I hope the loving dedication given to our animals, plants and the park itself comes shining through.

Wolfgang Kiessling
General Administrator

Our Setting: The Canary Islands

LORO PARQUE sparkles like a priceless gem set in the north of the Canary Islands. Although the Archipelago of seven volcanic islands lies directly off the north-west coast of Africa, politically the islands are an autonomous region of Spain. Through their links with Europe and Africa, the Canary Islands can be considered as a bridge between continents. From one of the islands - La Gomera - Christopher Columbus set sail on his voyage of discovery of the Americas.

Beautiful Puerto de la Cruz

On the north coast, in the valley of La Orotava, lies Puerto de la Cruz, with its balmy subtropical climate. The renowned explorer and scientist Alexander v. Humboldt wrote of the incredible impression this valley inspired when he first sighted t. The backdrop of the valley is the majestic volcano Teide, with an altitude of 3,718 metres, the highest mountain in Spain. The first travellers had already found their way to Puerto de la Cruz as early as the 17th century, thus establishing the town s a forerunner of tourism in the Canary Islands.

Puerto de la Cruz - a flourishing commercial port in the 19th century and a lively focus point for tourists to the Canaries since the middle of the 20th century, is the home of LORO PARQUE with the largest and most important collection of arrots in the world, Sealion show, Dolphin show, Parrot show, the largest Penguinarium in the world, Aquarium with Shark unnel, Gorillas, Chimpanzees, Tigers, Jaguars, Flamingos, Alligators, Tortoises, Orchid House, a "NATURAVISION" linema, the Gambian Market, Restaurants and many other attractions.

S. M.
LA REINA SIRIKIT DE THAILANDIA
VISITO LAS INSTALACIONES DEL LORO PARQUE
24 - 1 - 1996

The Kingdom of Thailand

As soon as you step into the magnificent Thai Pavillion at the main entrance, you will find yourself entering an exotic world of plants and animals from the five continents. In 1913 HRH Prince Mahidol, of Siam, father of the present King, HM King Bhumibol of Thailand, visited Tenerife. With masterly sketches and drawings he recorded the most spectacular landscapes of the island in his diary. The bust, at the entrance to the Thai Pavillion, in commemoration of his visit, also serves as a reminder of the strong links between Thailand, Tenerife and LORO PARQUE.

Almost 80 years later, his daughter, HRH Princess Galyani Vadhana, inaugurated the Thai Pavillion, the largest traditional Thai construction outside Thailand. The Princess on returning to the Royal Palace, was so enthusiastic about her visit, that her Majesty Queen Sirikit, following in the steps of her ancestors, also visited Tenerife and Loro Parque in 1996 accompanied by her entourage.

All elements of the six buildings are made of wood. The roof gables and ridges are decorated with 24 carat gold leaf and together with the roof tiles, were hand-made in Thailand by master craftsmen and erected on this site by specialists from Thailand.

Points to remember

Our visitors are always amazed at how well we care for LORO PARQUE. Please help us to maintain this high standard by respecting the following guidelines:
- Make use of the many **litter bins** and **ashtrays** which you find in the park
- Please dispose of your **chewing gum**
- **Nicotine** is detrimental to the health of animals
- Our animals have their own **special diet**. Please do not feed them
- Please **do not disturb** the animals. Restrict yourself to observing them
- Enjoy the **tranquility** of the park. Please do not bring your **radio** or make **excessive noise**
- **Dogs** are not permitted in LORO PARQUE
- The **barriers** are there for your own protection. Please remain on the paths
- Please feel free to take **photographs** and to **film**. However, the use of **flash** near the animals is not permitted
- For **commercial filming**, please obtain permission from the Management
- **Toilets** are located in the Thai Village, in the Picnic area, near the restaurant "Choza de los Duques", in the Jungle, at the Parrot Show and at "NATURAVISION" and Delfinario
- **Telephones**: in the Thai Village, in the Picnic area, at Loro Show, in the Jungle and at "NATURAVISION"
- **Wheelchairs** are obtainable at the front desk on payment of a refundable security deposit
- **Children's Buggies and Electric Wheelchairs** can be hired at a reasonable daily cost
- We ask that our guest be **appropriately dressed** for the Parque
- For all objects **lost or found** please contact the main gate

Opening hours:
Daily from 8.30 - 18.45 during the whole year
Last entry: 17.00

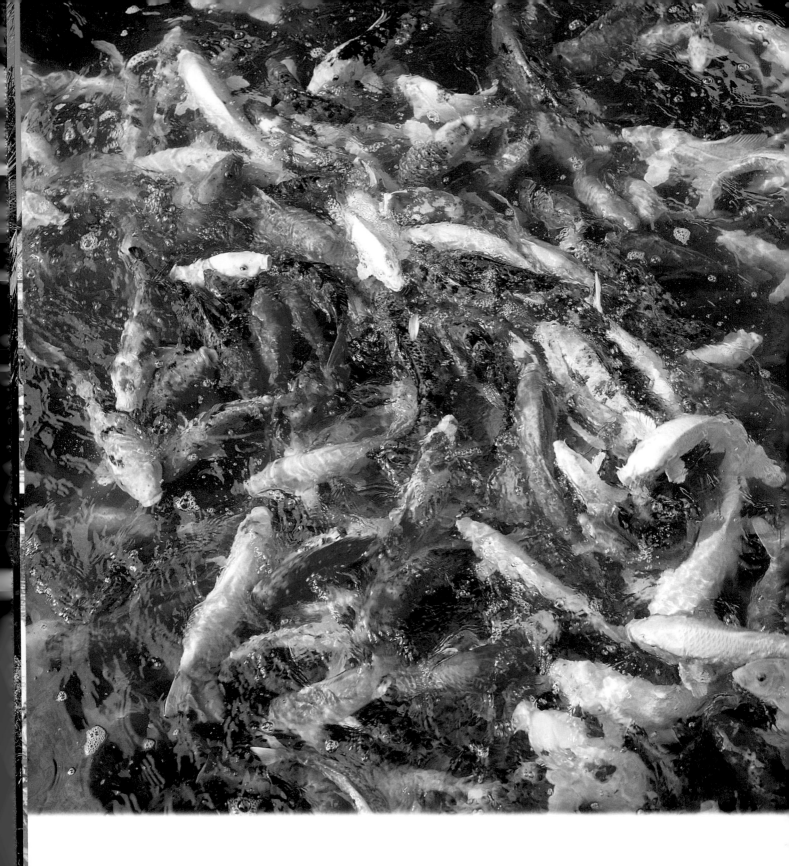

Koi Carp

The Thai Pavillion is set on a lake, home to a shoal of Japanese Koi Carp. These magnificent fish have been traditionally bred in Japan over hundreds of years with one goal: to breed a white Koi Carp with a single red mark on its breast - to symbolize the Japanese flag! At auctions in Japan, Koi Carp of attractive and unusual coloration find eager bidders for sums up to $100,000 and more.

Maayabu 28-07-88

Rafiki 29-05-91

Noel 28-12-86

Pole Pole 28-12-89

Schorsch 03-03-72

Pleasure without bars

Our gorilla terrace is unique, comprising an area of over 3.500 m^2 in which the animals roam freely over different levels amongst rich vegetation. Stop a while to observe the antics of these impressive apes as they swing from branches over a waterfall, relax or enjoy their vegetarian meals.

The five male gorillas housed here belong to different European zoos and form part of the European Breeding Programme for endangered Species (EEP) and the corresponding International Studbook (ISB). This programme is responsible for the coordination of the reproduction amongst Zoo gorillas, and its principal objective is to ensure a greater genetic variety within the European gorilla population, thus contributing to the conservation of this species which is endangered in the wild.

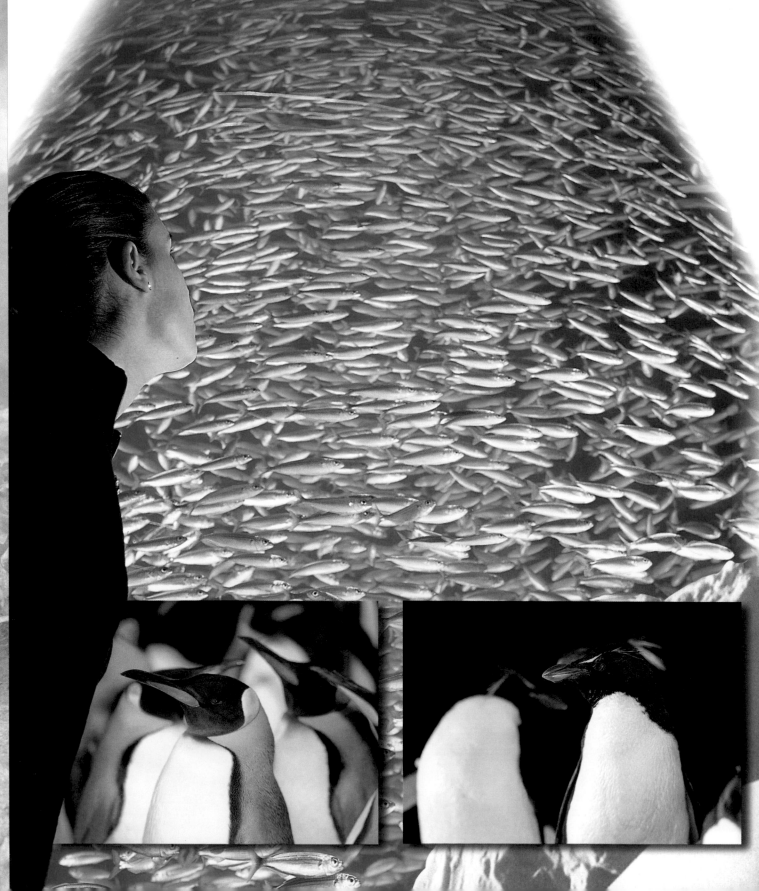

'Planet Penguin' offers to our visitors the unique opportunity to experience the wonders of the Antarctic in the largest reproduction ever built. Through a tunnel of ice they enter the most southern parts of our planet, discovered by man less than two centuries ago, although Ptolomeus had already predicted its existence more than 2000 years ago.

In the centre of the exhibit enclosed behind specially laminated glass panels, the characteristics of the antarctic climate have been perfectly reproduced. A rocky peninsula is the centre point, onto which 12 tons of snow fall daily. This is surrounded by 600 m³ of chilled sea water.

The exhibition portrays an unequalled setting for the Antarctic's most characteristic animal, the Penguin. The exhibit houses king penguins (Aptenodytes patagonicus), gentoo penguins (Pygoscelis papua), and rockhopper penguins (Eudyptes chrisocome). These species show the diversity of the whole penguin family, as well as their ability to adapt to the challenges of the harsh climate of the antarctic continent; The gentoo penguins, for example, build spectacular nests made of small stones on even ground, while the rockhopper penguins prefer inaccessible places such as precipices. There is no need for the king penguins to build nests - they incubate the eggs on their feet, being able to maintain the necessary temperature to keep them warm. Therefore, they even hatch their young on the ice surface. Within the installation, there is another exhibit which houses the subantarctic penguins, in this case the Humboldt penguins (Spheniscus humboldtii), a species threatened by extinction whose natural habitat are Peru's and Chile's subtropical, abundant fishing grounds; they build their nests digging into the soft ground or guano.

Visitors leave the exhibition following a spiral walkway around an acrylic cylinder, the biggest in the world over 8,5 m high and containing 100 m³ sea water and thousands of tiny fishes. Sunlight which is filtered through the surface is reflected by their scales creating the strange impression actually being submerged in the water itself.

Sea-lions (*Zalophus californianus*)

As you approach the futuristic roof design of the Californian sea-lion Theatre, the distinctive barks of these animals can be heard. The Sea-lion show is an absolute must. You will be amazed at the ease with which these intelligent marine mammals perform their fascinating acts.

Through transparent panels, they can also be observed under-water. Water is pumped through various filters into the 1,200,000 litre pool. The fact that they have successfully bred young is living proof that we have succeeded in our endeavour to make them feel at home. In 1996 the first baby sea lion was born, and since then another eleven pups have been brought into the world and today the sealion family consists of eighteen members. Children are always invited to participate in our shows, to give them the opportunity to experience direct contact with the animals.

PICNIC
VISTA TEIDE
TITÍS
DELFINARIO
RESTAURANT
LORO SHOW

Common Marmoset

(Callithrix jacchus)

LORO PARQUE has constructed a special place for this group of seven marmosets, very spacious and well-planted for them to be able to play and run. The visitors can observe the marmosets through the large glass panels and see how they play, catch flies, and eat the fruits and flowers of the plants that surround them. The Common Marmoset, unlike other primates, have claws on their fingers and toes instead of nails.

With an average weight of about 320g it is certainly one of the smallest New World primates.

Nearby you will find the Picnic-Area.

CHIMPLAND

A new home for the Chimpanzees *(Pan troglodytes)*

All our chimpanzees, with the exception of two youngsters born at LORO PARQUE, are animals rescued from street photographers. These photographers were only interested in the young, cuddly chimps and abandoned them to their fate when they matured and became difficult to manage. In the early 1980's, LORO PARQUE lovingly took these animals in and they moved to the chimpanzee enclosure, called CHIMPLAND. LORO PARQUE has gone to great pains to create a rocky environment for their needs in a 1,500 m^2 exhibit. From a cliff face in the south of the island a mould of latex and fibreglass was produced in a complex process. This mould was then transported to LORO PARQUE where it forms a frame for a cement structure with reinforced steel supports.

Inside the exhibit the individual artificial rocks are fused together to form a rocky cliff-face which, apart from being an attractive back-drop, at the same time creates a natural looking safe enclosure for the animals without any ugly wire netting or bars to obstruct the view.

The animals feel perfectly at home in this environment and the waterfall, ponds, cliffs and vegetation provide enough variety and scope for activity. The resting and sleeping area measures a generous 240 m^2 and caters for all the chimps' needs behind the scene.

You will delight in watching the comical behaviour of the chimps as they groom themselves. The large panorama windows offer ample opportunity to get a good view of the animals. The pink conspicuous hind-quarters of the females are a sign of sexual maturity. Chimpanzees have a life-span of about 35 years and in captivity tend to live even longer.

Prof. W. Köhler from Germany, who lived in Puerto de la Cruz from 1913 to 1920, was one of the first scientists to carry out behavioural studies on chimps and other primates.

Take a Break and Relax.

Coffee Shop "Vista Teide"

Self-service "Choza de los Duques"

Grill and Bar "Patio del Loro"

Pizzeria

Restaurant "Casa Pepe"

Café Flamingo

When you want a break and some refreshments,
we have a choice of restaurants:

The World's Largest Parrot Collection

These colourful and gregarious birds are predominantly found in the tropical rainforests. People love them for their beauty and intelligence, for which they have been hunted and captured, but commercial and environmental factors have also been their undoing. Of the more than 800 species and subspecies in the world, almost all are imperiled with extinction. For this reason captive breeding of endangered species can be a valuable tool in conservation.

LORO PARQUE houses the largest collection of parrots in the world, with over 340 species and subspecies. A total of some 3,000 parrots gives us an important genetic reserve for the many species threatened with extinction and belong to LORO PARQUE FOUNDATION (refer to the Appendix for a complete list of species).

Parrot Portrait

What makes parrots so unique?

Their plumage is their own special jewellery; for example,
long pointed tail-feathers or an erectile crest which
becomes prominent in display.

Their Size
The largest parrots are the Macaws. The magnificent Hyacinth
Macaw can reach a body length of up to 1 metre, while the
smallest the Pygmy Parrot (*micropsitta*)
measures just 8 cm.

The Feet
The feet of all parrots are zygodactyl, i.e. two toes point
forwards and two backwards. This allows parrots to grip
securely, enabling them to feed themselves with one foot
while standing on the other. When feeding in this manner
they bring the foot to their beak and not the reverse -
unique behaviour in the bird family.

The Beak
The large, curved beak is ideal for cracking seeds and nuts. To
clean it, parrots file their beak on branches and stones.

Language
Parrots have their own method of communication. However
in relationships with people they mimic
everything they hear, including human speech.

Family Life

Parrots are good parents and they mate for life. Here on the Canaries the height of the breeding season is from February to August and, depending on the species, a clutch of 1 to 10 eggs is laid. Eggs are incubated for 17 to 35 days, although this varies from species to species. During its first month, the completely naked and blind chick is normally cared for by the female, whilst the male provides food for the entire family. After 4 to 10 weeks, the young bird fledges, but remains with the parent birds for a certain time.

Tropical Parrots

Hawk-headed Parrot (*Deroptyus accipitrinus*)

You will be captivated by this much sought after parrot from the South American forests. It has a "collar" of feathers on its neck which, when ruffled or standing on end, creates a colourful fan of red tipped with light blue.

Red-lored Amazon
(*Amazona autumnalis autumnalis*)

Cuban Amazon
(*Amazona leucocephala*)

Amazons (*Amazona*)

Amazons originate from Central and South America and the Caribbean. Their plumage is predominantly green, which provides camouflage among the foliage. The individual species differ not only in size and colour, but also their beaks, wings and head feathers.

Amazons are popular pets, especially because of their ability to imitate voices and sound. Here in LORO PARQUE, we care for many Amazon species in danger of extinction in the wild due to the destruction of their natural habitats and illegal trade. LORO PARQUE houses the largest collection of Amazons in the world with over 40 species and subspecies.

Red-crowned Amazon
(*Amazona rhodocorytha*)

Blue-fronted Amazon
(*Amazona aestiva*)

Red-fronted Macaw
(*Ara rubrogenys*)

Scarlet Macaw
(*Ara macao*)

Macaws

Macaws are the largest of the parrots and inhabit South and Central America especially the rainforests and tropical wetlands. Some species can also be found in the savanna, riverlands and sub-tropical forests. These impressive birds owe their popularity, not only to their majestic appearance but also to their great intelligence and ability to mimic. Like all species of parrot, macaws are endangered and certain species are on the brink of extinction.

Blue and yellow Macaw
(*Ara ararauna*)

Military Macaw
(*Ara militaris*)

The Hyacinth Macaw (*Anodorhynchus hyacinthinus*)

These magnificent birds stand out not only because they are the largest of the parrots, capable of growing to a length of on metre, but also for their cobalt blue plumage contrasting with the yellow skin around the bill and eyes. In their natural habit f Central Brazil, they feed on fruit, berries and seeds as well as hard palm nuts and figs.

Red-headed painted Conure
(*Pyrrhua p. roseifrons*)

Pyrrhua

These adaptable parrots can be found in the forests and savannas of tropical and sub-tropical Central and South America. They have also been spotted at heights greater than 3.000 m. LORO PARQUE houses more than 15 species and subspecies of this genus.

Conures (*Aratinga* and *Guaruba*)

The conures are exclusive to Central and South America. The different species inhabit a wide variety of vegetation and climatic zones: rainforests, mangroves, humid, dry and thornbush savanna. The habitats vary according to the species. These birds are very intelligent and have a lovable personality.

Golden Conure
(*Guaruba guarouba*)

White-bellied and yellow-thighed Caique
(*Pionites l. leucogastaer, xanthomeria*)

Caique (*Pionites*)

The two species of this genus, which we have successfully bred, originate from the South American Amazon region. Their main characteristics are the white underparts.

Parrotlet (*Forpus*)

These parrotlets are one of the smallest of the parrot family, between 12 cm and 14.5 cm in size. They can be easily identified by their short tail feathers and, in most species, it is possible to distinguish the male from the female. The different species inhabit Central and South America and range from the rainforests to arid zones and from the lowlands to the mountains.

Yellow-faced Parrotlet
(*Forpus xanthops*)

Patagonian Conure (*Cyanoliseus Patagonus*)

The only species of this genus, the Patagonian Conure (*C. Patagonus*), makes its nest in the steep walls of cliffs or in the embankments of rivers. They live in small groups, even during the mating season and their colouration provides them with excellent camouflage.

Grey headed Parakeet (*Bolborhynchus*)

The chief characteristic of this small parakeet is its thick broad-sided bill. The photo shows the Aymara Parakeet (*Bolborhynchus aymara*) which originates in Central America and in the north-western part of South America. Loro Parque has had a great deal of success in breeding all of these species.

Purple-bellied Parrot (*Triclaria malachitacea*)

The Purple-bellied Parrot (*Triclaria malachitacea*) is the only representative of this genus which originates from south-eastern Brazil. It is rarely seen in captivity. The male can be easily distinguished from the female by the purple markings on the belly. LORO PARQUE houses the biggest population that exists in captivity is fortunate to have several breeding pairs which regularly produce young and is fortunate to have several breeding pairs which regularly produce young.

Pionus

This genus comprises eight species. They are predominantly green in colour but can be distinguished through variations in the colour of the head feathers. Pionus are native to the forests of Central and South America and bear a striking resemblance to their Amazon relatives. All of the species are on show at LORO PARQUE and the majority have been successfully bred. Photo: White-headed Pionus (*Pionus senilis*).

Short-tailed Parrots

(*Graydidascalus brachyurus*)

Their habitats are the rainforests of tropical South America. In captivity these birds are very seldom seen. 2001 LORO PARQUE saw the first successful breeding of these parrots.

Parakeet (*Brotogeris*)

This bird, which is native to South and Central America, has a distinctive narrow, extremely hooked bill, with which they can even remove snails from their shells in order to acquire essential proteins. Their plumage is almost entirely green, and serves as camouflage. All of the seven species of this genus live and breed at LORO PARQUE.

Inspired by the name of the Tui Parakeet (*Brotogeris sanctithomae sanctithomae*), which happily is not endangered, the large German Tour Operator TUI decided to make a very generous donation to LORO PARQUE FOUNDATION and thereby support our attempts to protect endangered parrot species.

Parrots

Ring-necked Parrot (*Psittacula*)

These attractive slender green parrots (*P. eupatria*) have remarkably colourful heads and long tails. They are expert flyers and, in most cases, the sexes can be distinguished by a difference in colouring. This is known as sexual dimorphism.

King Parrots (*Alisterus*)

They originate from Indonesia and some of these species are very similar to this Buru King Parrot.
Photo: (*Alisterus amboinensis buruensis*)

# of Asia

Hanging Parrots

(*Loriculus*)

These small lively birds take their name from their favourite resting and sleeping position: hanging upside-down like bats. They are mainly green in colour but have several markings and different colours on their head, throat and rump, giving them a multicoloured appearance. Here you can see the Blue-crowned Hanging-Parrot. (*Loriculus galgulus*).

Fig Parrots (*Psittaculirostris*)

This genus is a native of New Guinea. All three species are represented in our collection, of which *P. desmarestii* is the most colourful. This genus is relatively rare in captivity because they are difficult to care for. After some experimenting we have changed their diet, and have had extraordinary success in breeding and raising these birds.

Australian and Indonesian

Eastern Rosella
(*Platycercus eximius*)

Bourk's Parakeet
(*Neophema bourki*)

Timor-Crimson Red-winged Parakeet
(*Aprosmictus jonquillaceus*)

The huge Australian continent is home to many parrots of all colours. In spite of the severe climatological conditions in this area, these birds also thrive well in European climes. Numerous species of Cockatoos, Conures and Lories endemic to this region are very sought after by parrot lovers all over the world, and today in Europe you can find greater numbers of these birds than in their native country, thanks to captive breeding.

Parrots Conures and Lories

Red-collared Lorikeet
(*Trichoglossus h. rubritorquis*)

Rainbow Lory
(*Trichoglossus h. haematodus*)

Duivenbode's Lory
(*Chalcopsitta duivenbodei*)

There is nowhere in the world where you can admire as many species of lories as here in LORO PARQUE. These beautiful birds have one unique characteristic: their tongue has a hard tip on which there are tiny bristles. This is to enable the birds to collect pollen and nectar, their main source of nutrition. If you watch these birds while they eat, you can see this "brush" on the tip of their tongue

Goffin's Cockatoo
(*Cacatua goffini*)

Cockatoos

These large parrots are recognisable by their multi-coloured crests and their size. Their area of origin is very large, comprising the Philippines, Indonesia, Australia, Tasmania and the surrounding islands.

The head-crest of the impressive Major Mitchell's Cockatoo (*Cacatua leadbeateri*) from the Australian interior depicts the red and yellow stripes of the Spanish flag.

Blue-eyed Cockatoo
(*Cacatua ophthalmica*)

Major Mitchell's Cockatoo
(*Cacatua leadbeateri*)

Red-tailed Black-Cockatoo
(*Calyptorhynchus banksii*)

Massive exportation, the destruction of the forests and the greed of speculators have driven many cockatoos to the brink of extinction. Many large flocks of these birds can still be seen in Australia, thanks to a law passed in 1962 which punishes the disturbance of endemic animals with severe fines. LORO PARQUE houses 17 of the 18 species of cockatoo which exist.

Palm Cockatoo
(*Probosciger aterrimus*)

Yellow-tailed Black-Cockatoo
(*Calyptorhynchus funereus*)

Keas (*Nestor notabilis*)

This unusual species of parrot from the mountains of New Zealand bears a strong resemblance to the early parrots. They have a lively, playful nature and it is worth watching them at play for a while. They can often be seen rolling little stones into the pond with the aid of a stick - like little golfers!

The number of Keas in the wild has been decimated through persecution, because it was claimed that Keas attack and kill sheep. This belief is due to the fact that they were occasionally seen feeding on sheep carcasses.

The Keas are breeding regularly in LORO PARQUE.

Pesquet Parrots (*Psittrichas fulgidus*)

This parrot from New Guinea is so completely different from all other parrots that it is believed to be the closest to the original form of parrot. They are a rare treasure in any parrot collection. They eat only soft fruit, flowers and nectar. Pesquet parrots are rarely found in captivity and they are difficult to breed. LORO PARQUE has had more success in breeding these wonderful birds than any other zoo or private collection.

Aviaries

Utmost care has been taken in the design and construction of our aviaries. Thirty years of experience have taught us what our charges like most: free-standing aviaries, surrounded by vegetation, thus providing protection against the wind as well as natural screening from the other aviaries. As perches, we use natural tree branches which fits the particular needs of the parrots. The floor of the aviaries is covered with volcanic slag, which is both hygienic and controls the level of humidity in the air. The ropes and swings help our parrots with better co-ordination.

Once a week the Forestry Department supplies us with fresh pine-cones gathered when cleaning the underbrush. Whilst the birds are busy playing and nibbling the cones, they at the same time supplementing their diet. Since parrots have a great destructive tendency, interior planting of the aviaries is not recommended. Most of the birds are housed in such a way that the visitor can observe the animals without any optical barriers.

Cactus and other plants

In the Cactus Garden you can enjoy a magnificent collection of cactus and other succulents. In the course of evolution and adaption to a hostile environment the original foilage of these plants has developed into a protective cover of prickly thorns.

There are also different species of flowers to be seen throughout the park with colourful flowerbeds stretching over large green areas.

Also worth mentioning are the magnificent lawns and a wide range of annuals which can be seen in flower at any time of the year. There are more than 8.000 palms and many of the most attractive are represented at LORO PARQUE making a decorative addition to our gardens. Palm trees can be found in many parts of the world, from equatorial and other tropical forests, to the moderate climes of the Mediterranean.

Canarian Flora

An interesting representation of Canarian flora is also to be found i
the park, including the Canarian Palm and the magnificent *Euphorbi*
canariensis, which are planted in volcanic stones covering an area o
50 m² and you can also find the Dragon Trees (*Dracaena draco*).

This tree is a species endemic to the Canary Islands. The loca
population used the sap to make a red dye which they nickname
"Dragon's blood". These trees are extremely long-lived and can exis
for a thousand years.

NATURAVISION

Visit our cinema set in a specially-built theatre with its impressive mirrored dome, and let yourself be swept away to some of the most breath-taking beauty spots in the world with our film "NATURAVISION".

Pass through the tropical rain forests of the Amazon on a boat and observe the crocodiles as they hunt, as well as monkeys and other inhabitants of the jungle. Fly through unexplored deep gorges or over enormous table mountains filled with countless waterfalls. Discover the fauna and flora of the Spanish National Parks or dive in the colourful coral reefs teeming with exotic fish. Thanks to its special "Showscan" technology and digital sound, our film "NATURAVISION", first shown in 1992 at EXPO in Seville, is an unforgettable experience.

orquidario

The Chinese philosopher Confucius hailed the orchid as "queen of the scented plants". You will fully understand his sentiments when you vist the orchid house at LORO PARQUE. A delicate scent lingers in the air whilst you marvel at the richness of form and colour of these most elegant flowers.

There are more than 25.000 different species of orchid. In no other plant family has it been possible to produce so many hybrids. In the last 125 years, more than 75 000 hybrids have been named. For this reason, the Royal Horticultural Society has founded an international commision which controls and legalizes the naming of each new hybrid. At any time of the year you will find orchids from all over the world, such as *Cambria, Cattleya, Cymbidium, Dendrobien, Laelia, Miltonia, Odontoglossum, Phalaenopsis* and *Vanden* in blossom at LORO PARQUE.

The Alligators (Alligátor mississippensis)

The Mississippi-Alligator which has a round and wide snout distinguishing in from the Cayman, can grow up to a length of 4 to 6 metres. Our Alligators have already reached 2 metres. Their home in the Parque has a Ficus Rubiginosa tree for a roof and a mass of enormous Birds of Paradise flowers for its walls and apart from this there is a wonderfurl view from here of the sea and the Dragon Trees.

The exhibit has a hcating system for the sand of their beach and the water, so this way the Alligators can always find their own individual ideal temperature

Jaguar (*Panthera onca*)

The black female and his yellow spotted male live in a crater-like landscape planted with trees, lush vegetation, a brook and a pond. At times, when stopping to watch these majestic animals behind the large panorama windows, one cannot help but wonder if it is not the onlooker who is the actual object of observation...

Loro-Show

When LORO PARQUE first opened to the public more than 30 years ago, this was the only parrot show in Europe. The new Loro theatre is also the venue for the Free-flying show - an enthralling colourful presentation of macaws in full flight. These winged artists offer you an unforgettable performance.

The Galapagos Tortoise
(*Geochelone nigra*)

Before reaching Tiger Island, stop by the enclosure of the Galapagos Tortoises. This species has suffered great decimation over the last decades. Already in the times of the early whaling ships these giant tortoises were easy prey, when crews stocked up with fresh tortoise meat as a food reserve on their long voyages.
Tom is approximately 40 years old and weighs some 90 kilos. He is gentle and sluggish and lives on fruit, vegetables and leaves of the *opuntia* cactus - thorns and all!

Tiger Island

Some days ago two new inhabitants arrived to Tiger Island, two beautiful *siberian* tigers named Prince and *Saba*. Prince is a young male, born three years ago in the *Jerez* Zoo, while *Saba* is a seven year old tigress born in Barcelona Zoo. But Prince is also an unusual tiger because of his skin, which does not have the common yellow, orange and black coloration, but is totally white with some grey stripes. There are a few individuals of albinos tiger in the world, as this coloration is caused by a strange genetic mutation favoured by the captive breeding.

Both individuals were property of a private owner, and they were used in shows in *Mallorca* Island. LORO PARQUE offered the owner its extraordinary facilities to give a more relaxed and adequate future for this big cats. Prince and *Saba* are successfully going through the process of adaptation to their new home, and since some weeks they can be seen in the Tiger Island by all our visitors.

Happy Dolphins

It is a beautiful sight to see these marine mammals (Tursiops truncatus) living so happily in the biggest, most natural and most attractive dolphinarium in Europe. The installations were constructed using the most advanced technology possible to create the optimun conditions for their happiness, growthand reproduction.

You can enjoy the wonderful artistic displays that these dolphins, as well as their frollicking four babies that in some cases like to accompany their mothers, give us. The presence of these four delightful playful youngsters is proof indeed that the dolphins are happy at LORO PARQUE.

The dolphinarium has a capacity of 7.000.000 litres, divided into the main exhibition pool, the holdings or quarantine pools, and a panoramic pool with transparent sides.

The water is purified using an electrolytic process that does not involve any chemicals, rather it uses the natural chlorine from the sea water itself.

The seating capacity is for 1.500 spectators, and the show is full of unforgettable moments.

delfinario

Charlie Chaplin

In his comical way
"Charlie Chaplin", dearly loved by young and
old, entertains the visitors
to the dolphinarium.

Gambian Market

Stroll through the bazar and souvenir shops
of this realistic representation of a Gambian Market
and let yourself get carried away by the colourful
African atmosphere.
Enjoy refreshing exotic drinks and snacks at the African
bar and take a genuine Gambian souvenir home with you.

Children's Playground

Here, our young visitors (for ages up to 9 years) can let off steam, and the variety of activity and play has made this a popular stop-over for parents and children alike and, whilst keeping a watchful eye on their youngsters, parents can enjoy a relaxing drink at the nearby kiosk or in the restaurant "Casa Pepe".

Parque infantil

César Manrique

We would like to honour a friend - the great and unique Canarian artist and landscape architect, César Manrique, for his great contribution to the Canary Islands and LORO PARQUE.

The Coral Reef

Every one of the corals here on show in the aquarium is a living colony of tiny organisms, which in certain cases construct a calcified exoskeleton using the various dissolved carbonates in the sea water. These corals can take an infinite variety of forms, designs and colours and may even group together and form coral reefs, extending for several thousands of kilometers.

The bigger fish are housed in an aqarium with artificial coral meanwhile up to 40 different types of coral and tropical fish may be obscrved in the aquarium at opposite.

Thai Village 1
Koi Carps 2
Gorillas 3
Planet Penguin 4
SHOW Sea lions 5
Marmosets 6
Chimpland 7
Pelicans 8
Macaw Jungle 9
Baby Station 10
Natura Vision 11
Flamingoes 12
Orchid House 13
Aligators 14
Jaguars 15
Cranes 16
Loro Show 17
Fantasy Foto 18
African Market 19
Sea Lions 20
Giant Tortoise 21
Tiger Island 22
Dolphin Show 23
Lories 24
Childrens Playground 25
Aquarium 26
Porcelaine Museum 27

"VISTA TEIDE" I

PIZZERIA & SELF SERVICE "CHOZA DE LOS DUQUES" II

"CASA PEPE" III

GRILL & BAR "PATIO DEL LORO" IV

RESTA...

CAFE

NATURA VISION

15 16 13 14 12 10 11 9

BAR

TOILETS

CASH-POINT

INFORMATION

BABY CHANGE

TELEPHONES

PIC-NIC

BOUTIQUES

LORO PARQUE
Fundacion

Avda. Venezuela - LORO PARQUE - Avda. Venezuela
Free Express every 20 mins.
LAST DEPARTURE LORO PARQUE - Avda. Venezuela at 18:45 h.

Biology of the Grey-headed Parrot

Total Support by LPF (until 2002):   US$ 5,000

The Grey-headed Parrot Poicephalus fuscicollis suahelicus, is found in some parts of South Africa, Zimbabwe, Mozambique, Namibia, Angola, Zambia, Tanzania, Burundi, Rwanda and the Central African Republic. Its conservation status is undetermined and very little is known of its biology in the wild. The Loro Parque Fundación decided to support research by Craig Symes into the biology of the Grey-headed Parrot, as this will determine the status of the species in the wild and form a basis for future conservation strategies.

The principal objectives of the project are to establish and map the historic and present day distribution; to model the abundance on a temporal and spatial scale; to describe the breeding biology; to identify breeding requirements; to identify feeding and habitat requirements and estimate food availability.

Conservation of Endemic Parrots on Tanimbar-Islands Indonesia

Total Support by LPF (until 2002)   US$ 23,800

Given that a National Park is due to be declared on the island of Halmahera -subsequent to survey work supported by Loro Parque Fundación- the Tanimbar Islands are presently regarded as the highest priority in eastern Indonesia as regards the need for protected area gazettement.

Loro Parque Fundación financed the first phase of this project, aimed at determining the status, habitat use and traffic in Goffin's Cockatoo *(Cacatua goffini) and the Blue-streaked Lory* (Eos reticulata). Whereas the results show that the populations of both species are stable, seemingly being able to compensate the loss of numbers both from natural mortality and from illegal trade, the project implementors also emphasised that pressure exerted by logging companies has started to take effect on the island,

Red-vented Cockatoo Conservation Programme
(Cacatua haematuropygia)

Total Support by LPF (until 2002):   US$ 73,611

The endemic Philippine or Red-vented Cockatoo is increasingly approaching the brink of extinction due to large-scale habitat loss and intense poaching activities. Formerly occurring throughout the Philippine archipelago, it is now reduced to an estimated 750-2000 individuals, with the largest remaining populations today found on Palawan and adjacent smaller islands.

The activities, which fully involve the local communities, continued on the small offshore island of Rasa. A wardening scheme on this island, which has the densest cockatoo population known to remain, ensured that no nests were poached. About 19 birds could be added to the local population, which is estimated at 60 birds and expected to re-colonise the mainland of Palawan soon.

Protection of Phu Khieo Wildlife Sanctuary

Total Support by LPF (until 2002):   US$ 170,656

Since 1997, the Loro Parque Fundación has been collaborating with the Royal Forest Department of Thailand to assist in the conservation of Phu Khieo Wildlife Sanctuary (PKWS), which is one of the most important protected areas in north-eastern Thailand, and the third largest wildlife sanctuary in the country as a whole.

The project has included a wide range of activities, such as biodiversity surveys, GIS resource mapping, as well as community awareness and environmental education programmes. To further promote the project, the LPF also decided to finance the participation of one Royal Forestry Department staff member in a one-year course in Conservation Education, newly given by RARE Center for Tropical Conservation at the Durrell Institute of Conservation and Ecology at the University of Kent.

Hotel Botánico

The Leading Hotel of the World

another highlight in Puerto de la Cruz

During 1995, THE LORO PARQUE GROUP purchased the Hotel Botánico, and set about totally refurbishing and remodeling it, to recreate a Great Luxury Hotel of world wide fame. It is now one of the Leading Hotels of the World, and as such makes it somewhere special to spend the holiday of your dreams. It sits in its own oasis of 25.000 m² of tropical gardens, there are 250 rooms and 12 suites, swimming pools with a jacuzzi, restaurants that serve a wide variety of local and international dishcs, plus a health and beauty centre.
There are congress facilities for up to 500 people, everything you require to ensure a successful stay.

one of
The Leading Hotels of the World ®

1997: **Gold Medal Award**	Tour Operator:	Thomson Holidays, England "Best a la carte accomodation"
1998: **Gold Medal Award**	Tour Operator:	Thomson Holidays, England "Best a la carte accomodation"
1998: **"Best Resort Hotel of Spain"**	Tour Operator:	Magic Travel Group, England
1998: **"Holly" Award**	Tour Operator:	TUI, Germany
1999: **"Holly" Award**	Tour Operator:	TUI, Germany
2000: **Gastronomy Award**	Tour Operator:	Pegase, Belgium
2001: **Gastronomy Award**	Tour Operator:	Pegase, Belgium
2001: **Environment Quality Award**	Hotel Association:	Ashotel, Tenerife, Spain
2001: **"Biosphere Hotels**	UNESCO-ITR: Spain	Institute of Responsible Tourism,
2001: **Environment Quality Award**	Tour Operator: :	Kuoni, Switzerland
2001: **Environment Quality Award**	Tour Operator: :	Hotelplan, Switzerland
2001: **Gold Medal Award**	Tour Operator:	Thomson Holidays, England "Best a la carte accomodation"
2002: **"Holly" Award**	Tour Operator:	TUI, Germany
2002: **Gastronomy Award**	Tour Operator:	Pegase, Belgium

We are at your service, to do the very best we can, to make your visit a most memorable one. Satisfied customers. coming back to visit us fine time and time again, is our best recommendation.

Until the next time!

LORO PARQUE

Behind
the scenes

Join us on our entertaining and educational
Discovery Tour which will take you "Behind the
Scenes" of the Parque to show you a little of
what it takes to successfully run such a diverse
facility. We will tell you all about our animals
and birds, including some amusing stories
about them. We will show you machine rooms,
quarantine areas, sleeping quarters and tell
you the history of the Parque, how it has grown
over the years and about the people who
made the dream into a reality.

The tour lasts one and half hours and operates every day of the week in Spanish, German and English.
For a nominal charge we will help make your visit to Loro Parque even more enjoyable than you thought
possible.

Parrots (species and subspecies)

Agapornis canus
Agapornis fischeri
Agapornis lilianae
Agapornis nigrigenis
Agapornis personata
Agapornis pullaria
Agapornis roseicollis
Agapornis taranta
Alisterus a. dorsalis
Alisterus a. amboinensis
Alisterus a. buruensis
Alisterus a. hypophonius
Alisterus c. moszkowskii
Alisterus s. scapularis
Amazona a. aestiva
Amazona a. xanthopteryx
Amazona agilis
Amazona a. albifrons
Amazona a. nana
Amazona amazonica
Amazona arausiaca
Amazona a. autumnalis
Amazona a. diadema
Amazona a. lilacina
Amazona a. salvini
Amazona barbadensis
Amazona brasiliensis
Amazona collaria
Amazona dufresniana
Amazona rhodocorytha
Amazona f. farinosa
Amazona f. guatemalae
Amazona f. bodini
Amazona f. festiva
Amazona finschi
Amazona guildingii
Amazona m. mercenaria
Amazone mercenaria canipalliata
Amazona l. leucocephala
Amazona o. auropalliata
Amazona o. nattereri
Amazona o. ochrocephala
Amazona o. oratrix
Amazona o. caribae
Amazona o. panamensis
Amazona o. parvipes
Amazona o. tresmariae
Amazona o. xantholaema
Amazona pretrei
Amazona tucumana
Amazona ventralis
Amazona vinacea
Amazona viridigenalis
Amazona xantholora
Amazona xanthops
Anodorhynchus hyacinthinus
Aprosmictus erythropterus
Aprosmictus jonquillaceus
Ara ambigua
Ara ararauna
Ara auricollis
Ara chloroptera
Ara couloni
Ara glaucogularis
Ara macao
Ara manilata
Ara maracana
Ara m. militaris
Ara n. cumanensis
Ara n. nobilis
Ara rubrogenys
Ara severa
Aratinga a. acuticaudata
Aratinga a. haemorhous
Aratinga aurea
Aratinga auricapilla
Aratinga cactorum
Aratinga c. canicularis
Aratinga c. eburnirostrum
Aratinga c. clarae
Aratinga chloroptera
Aratinga erythrogenys
Aratinga euops
Aratinga finschi
Aratinga jandaya

Aratinga holochlora
Aratinga rubritorquis
Aratinga solstitialis
Aratinga leucophthalmus
Aratinga mitrata
Aratinga n. astec
Aratinga n. nana
Aratinga p. pertinax
Aratinga p. surinama
Aratinga w. frontata
Aratinga weddellii
Barnardius b. barnardi
Barnardius b. macgillivrayi
Barnardius z. semitorquatus
Barnardius z. zonarius
Bolborhynchus aymara
Bolborhynchus lineola
Bolborhynchus a. aurifrons
Bolborhynchus a. robertsi
Bolborhynchus orbygnesius
Brotogeris c. beniensis
Brotogeris c. cyanoptera
Brotogeris c. chrysopterus
Brotogeris c. tuipara
Brotogeris jugularis
Brotogeris v. versicolorus
Brotogeris v. chiriri
Brotogeris pyrrhopterus
Brotogeris tirica
Brotogeris sanctithomae
Cacatua alba
Cacatua ducorpsii
Cacatua g. eleonora
Cacatua g. galerita
Cacatua g. triton
Cacatua goffini
Cacatua haematuropygia
Cacatua leadbeateri
Cacatua moluccensis
Cacatua ophthalmica
Cacatua pastinator
Cacatua s. abotti
Cacatua s. sulphurea
Cacatua s. sanguinea
Cacatua s. citrinocristata
Cacatua tenuirostris
Callocephalon fimbriatum
Calyptorhynchus f. baudini
Calyptorhynchus f. funereus
Calyptorhynchus magnificus
Chalcopsitta a. atra
Chalcopsitta a. bernsteini
Chalcopsitta a. insignis
Chalcopsitta cardinalis
Chalcopsitta duivenbodei
Chalcopsitta scintillata
Charmosyna josephinae
Charmosyna multistriata
Charmosyna p. goliathina
Charmosyna p. placentis
Charmosyna p. subplacens
Charmosyna pulchella
Charmosyna rubronotata
Coracopsis nigra
Coracopsis v. vasa
Coracopsis v. drouhardi
Cyanoliseus p. patagonus
Cyanoliseus p. andinus
Cyanoliseus p. bloxami
Cyanopsitta spixii
Cyanoramphus auriceps
Cyanoramphus novaezelandiae
Deroptyus a. accipitrinus
Deroptyus a. fuscifrons
Eclectus r. aruensis
Eclectus r. polychloros
Eclectus r. roratus
Eclectus r. solomonensis
Eclectus r. vosmaeri
Eclectus r. riedeli
Eclectus r. cornelia
Enicognathus ferrugineus
Enicognathus leptorhynchus
Eolophus roseicapilla
Eos b. cyanonothus

Eos bornea
Eos cyanogenia
Eos histrio
Eos reticulata
Eos semilarvata
Eos s. squamata
Eos s. obiensis
Eos s. riciniata
Eos s. atrocaerulea
Eunymphicus c. cornutus
Forpus coelestis
Forpus conspicillatus
Forpus cyanopygius
Forpus passerinus
Forpus p. deliciosus
Forpus p. viridissimus
Forpus spengeli
Forpus xanthops
Forpus x. flavissimus
Forpus x. xanthopterygius
Glosopsitta concinna
Graydidascalus brachyurus
Guarouba guarouba
Lathamus discolor
Loriculus galgulus
Loriculus philippensis
Loriculus stigmatus
Loriculus vernalis
Lorius chlorocercus
Lorius domicellus
Lorius garrulus
Lorius g. flaviopalliatus
Lorius g. morataianus
Lorius lory
Lorius l. salvadori
Lorius l. erythrothorax
Melopsittacus undulatus
Myiopsitta monachus
Nandayus nenday
Neophema crhysostoma
Neophema bourki
Neophema elegans
Neophema pulchella
Neophema splendida
Neopsittacus musschenbroekii
Neopsittacus pullicauda
Nestor notabilis
Nymphicus hollandicus
Opopsitta diophthalma
Opopsitta gulielmiterti
Opopsitta g. amabilis
Oreopsittacus arfaki major
Pionites l. leucogaster
Pionites l. xanthomeria
Pionites melanocephala
Pionopsitta pileata
Pionus chalcopterus
Pionus fuscus
Pionus maximiliani
Pionus menstruus
Pionus s. corallinus
Pionus senilis
Pionus seniloides
Pionus tumultuosus
Platycercus a. adscitus
Platycercus a. palliceps
Platycercus a. adelaidae
Platycercus a. subadelaide
Platycercus caledonicus
Platycercus elegans
Platycercus eximius
Platycercus flaveolus
Platycercus icterotis
Platycercus venustus
Poicephalus cryptoxanthus
Poicephalus g. gulielmi
Poicephalus g. fantiensis
Poicephalus g. massaicus
Poicephalus meyeri
Poicephalus r. fuscicollis
Poicephalus rueppellii
Poicephalus rufiventris
Poicephalus senegalus
Poicephalus s. mesotypus
Polytelis alexandrae

Polytelis anthopeplus
Polytelis swainsonii
Prioniturus mada
Prosciger a. aterrimus
Prosciger a. goliath
Prosopeia t. tabuensis
Prosopeia splendens
Psephotus c. chrysopterygius
Psephotus c dissimilis
Psephotus h. haematogaster
Psephotus h. haematorrhous
Psephotus haematonotus
Psephotus varius
Pseudeos fuscata
Psittacula a. abotti
Psittacula a. alexandri
Psittacula calthorpae
Psittacula columboides
Psittacula cyanocephala
Psittacula derbyana
Psittacula e. siamensis
Psittacula eupatria
Psittacula h. finschii
Psittacula himalayana
Psittacula k. krameri
Psittacula k. manillensis
Psittacula longicauda
Psittacula roseata
Psittaculirostris desmarestii
Psittaculirostris edwardsii
Psittaculirostris salvadori
Psittacus e. erithacus
Psittacus e. timneh
Psittinus cyanurus
Psittrichas fulgidus
Purpureicephalus spurius
Pyrrhura cruentata
Pyrrhura egregia
Pyrrhura frontalis
Pyrrhura hoffmanni gaudens
Pyrrhura l. leucotis
Pyrrhura l. emma
Pyrrhura l. griseipectus
Pyrrhura m. melanura
Pyrrhura m. pacifica
Pyrrhura m. souancei
Pyrrhura m. molinae
Pyrrhura m. restricta
Pyrrhura m. hypoxantha
Pyrrhura p. coerulescens
Pyrrhura p. lepida
Pyrrhura p. perlata
Pyrrhura p. picta
Pyrrhura p. roseifrons
Pyrrhura rhodocephala
Pyrrhura r. rupicola
Pyrrhura r. sandiae
Rhynchopsitta pachyrhyncha
Tanygnathus lucionensis
Tanygnathus megalorhynchus
Tanygnathus sumatranus
Trichoglossus chlorolepidotus
Trichoglossus euteles
Trichoglossus f. flavoviridis
Trichoglossus f. meyeri
Trichoglossus goldiei
Trichoglossus h. capistratus
Trichoglossus h. ceruliceps
Trichoglossus h. djampeanus
Trichoglossus h. forsteni
Trichoglossus h. haematodus
Trichoglossus h. massena
Trichoglossus h. mitchelli
Trichoglossus h. moluccanus
Trichoglossus h. rosenbergii
Trichoglossus h. rubritorquis
Trichoglossus h. stresemanni
Trichoglossus h. weberi
Trichoglossus iris
Trichoglossus j. johnstoniae
Trichoglossus ornatus
Triclaria malachitacea
Vini australis

Tropical Marine Fishes

Aeanthurus achilles
Acanthurus japonicus
Acanthurus leucosternon
Acanthurus lineatus
Amphiprion clarkii
Amphiprion melanopus
Amphiprion percula
Amphiprion perideraion
Amphiprion rubrocinctus
Anisotremus virginicus
Antennarius sp.
Arothron meleagris
Balistoides conspicillum
Canthigaster sp.
Centropyge bicolor
Centropyge bispinosus
Centropyge flavissimus
Centropyge loriculus
Chaetodon collare
Chaetodon auriga
Chaetodon falcula
Chaetodon fasciatus
Chaetodon mertensii
Chaetodon miliaris
Chaetodon pauifasciatus
Chaetodon pelewensis
Chaetodenuis pencilligerus
Chaetodon semilarvatus
Chaetodontoplus duboulayi
Chelmon rostratus
Chilomycterus schoepfi
Chromis viridis
Chrysiptera parasema
Ctenochaetus striatus
Dascyllus trimacula
Dascyllus aruanus
Dascyllus melanurus
Diodon holacauthus
Ecsenius bicolor
Euxiphipops xanthometopon
Forcipiger flavissimus
Gnathanodon speciosus
Gramma loreto
Heniochus acuminatus
Hippocampus reidi
Holacanthus ciliaris
Holacanthus tricolor
Labroides dimidiatus
Lactoria cornuta
Lienardella fasciata
Lo vulpines
Lutjanus sebae
Naso brevirostris
Naso brevirostris
Naso lituratus
Naso vlamingi
Nemateleotris decora
Nemateleotris magnifica
Odonus niger
Paracanthurus hepatus
Parachaetodon ocellatus
Parupeneus cyclostomus
Plataxteira
Plectorhinchus chaetodonoides
Pomacanthus annularis
Pomacanthus arcuatus
Pomacanthus imperator
Pomacanthus maculosus
Pomacanthus paru
Pomacentrus pavo
Premnas braculeatus
Pseudanthias squamipinnis
Ptereleotris evides
Ptereleotris zebra
Pteroapogon kauderni
Pterois antennata
Pterois volitans
Pterosynchiropus splendidus
Rhinecanthus aculeatus
Salarias sp.
Selene vomer
Serranocirrhitus latus
Symphorichthys spilurus
Synchiropus picturatus
Thalassoma lunare
Valenciennea strigata
Zanclus cornutus
Zebrasoma desjardinii
Zebrasoma flavescens
Zebrasoma xanthurum

Canarian Fishes

Abudefduf luridus
Aluterus scriptus
Diplodus cervinus cervinus
Diplodus puntazzo
Diplodus sargus cardenati
Diplodus vulgaris
Enchelycore anatina
Epinephelus guaza
Gymnothorax unicolor
Lithognathus mormyrus
Muraena augusti
Muranea helena
Mycteroperca rubra
Paraprisoma cretense
Parapristipoma octolineatum
Pomadasys incisus
Pseudolepidaplois scrofa
Sarpa salpa
Serramus scriba
Sparisoma cretense
Sphoeroides spengleri
Thalassoma pavo
Trachinotus ovatus
Xyrichthys novacula

Sharks and Rays

Carchahinus melanopterus
Carcharhinus plumbeus
Chiloscyllium punctatum
Dasyatis americana
Ginglymostroma cirratum
Odontaspis taurus
Stegostoma fasciatum
Triakis semifasciatum

Invertebrate

Actinodiscus sp.
Anemonia
Cladiella species
Clibanarius aequabilis
Heteractis
Lysmata grahami
Octopus vulgaris
Paracucumaria sp.
Sarcophyton acutangulum
Sinularia sp.
Stenorhynchus lanceolatus
Zoanthus sp.

Fresh Water Fishes

Barbodes schwanenfeldii
Cichlasoma bifasciatum
Cichlasoma citrinellum
Cichlasoma dovii
Cichlasoma friedrichsthalii
Cichlasoma guttulatum
Cichlasoma maculicauda
Cichlasoma temporalis
Colossoma macroponum
Coris formosa
Corydoras aeneus
Ctenopoma acutirostre
Cyphotilapia frontosa
Cyprichromis leptosoma
Haplochromis moorii
Haplochromis fenestratus
Haplochromis chrysonotus
Haplochromis compressiceps
Haplochromis electra
Haplochromis milomo
Haplochromis moorii
Hemichromis cristatus
Hypostomus plecostomus
Inlidichromis transcriptus
Inlidochromis regani
Julidochromis transcriptus
Julidochromis regani
Labeotropheus fuelleborni
Lamprologus brevis
Lamprologus brichrardi
Lamprologus calvus
Lamprologus cylindricus
Lamprologus leleupi
Lamprologus tretocephalus
Melanochromis johanni
Melanochromis sp
Ophthalmotilapia ventralis
Conydoras axelrodi
Osphronemus goramy
Osteoglossum bicirrhosum
Haplocromis electra
Potamotrygon leopoldi
Potamotrygon motoro
Pseudotropheus elongatus
Pseudotropheus crabro
Pseudotropheus lombardoi
Pseudotropheus zebra
Serrasalmus nattereri
Symphysodon s.p.
Synodontis decorus
Synodontis multipunctatus
Tetraodon mbu
Tropheus duboisi